Phyllis Kuehnl-Walters, Ph.D.

Worry, Fret, and Fear... No More!

A Six-Week Challenge to Eliminate Worry and
Overcome Your Fears

Worry, Fret, and Fear… No More!

Copyright © 2018 by Phyllis Kuehnl-Walters

ISBN 978-1-976-88724-6

First printing January 2018 / Printed in the United States of America

For my husband, Dan Walters, whose love and encouragement to write this book has been unceasing.

And to my son, Eric Kuehnl, without whose support this endeavor may not have been completed.

God bless you both in running your race as you have allowed me to run mine.

Preface:
Worry, Fret, and Fear... No More!

In these six weeks, you will be taught to eliminate worrying and fearful thoughts from your life. You will be encouraged to change your negative thoughts and feelings. This book will lead you through Bible verses and present strategies that have worked for many people including my clients, family, friends, students, and myself.

For the past seven years, I have taught workshops, primarily for Senior Citizens, regarding the challenges they must face in order to successfully adapt to life changes, planned and unforeseen. I have shared what has worked for me in my bleakest times and I will now share my insight with you.

I have spent forty years as a clinical Psychologist in private practice. My clients represented diverse populations ranging from male and female prison inmates to well–known and respected judges, lawyers, doctors, stay-at-home parents, single parents, couples, and business people. These people were not all Christians. But they were motivated by a desire to live their lives according to Judeo-Christian principles.

For myself, I have also been blessed with opportunities to volunteer for short–term mission trips to Zambia, Austria, Appalachia, and American Indian reservations. These trips have broken down many of my barriers that created fear of the unknown and worry about things from which only God can protect me. As a result, my energy has become more directed and my insecurities overcome. Who am I to be sent to such places? I believe God has placed me here for such a time as this. I feel that it is my calling to write to you and offer you a future without worry or fear.

Setbacks may occur, but you must believe that they are simply setups for a more fruitful future. A future without limitations!

I hope you take the challenge. You won't regret it.

Phyllis

Contents

Introduction

As a Christian Psychologist, the strategies that I encourage you to implement are based upon The Word of God. You will be lead through a series of small steps each day. Each week, you will be presented with five short Bible verses and my commentaries. I also ask that you journal your own daily written responses or use the space provided.

You will be taught to seek answers by developing new habits such as attending church, reading the Bible, keeping a gratitude journal and a prayer journal, reading daily devotionals and other Christian materials, watching Christian television, listening to inspirational music, attending a weekly Bible study, being mentored by an accountability partner, and trusting the Lord.

As you answer the questions that follow each day's scripture and personal commentary, you will begin demonstrating the self-discipline needed to modify your negative, worrisome, fearful thoughts and therefore your behavior.

On the weekend, I ask that you intentionally apply a Godly principle that touched your heart this week. To go deeper, you can complete the written challenge and pray for direction in the coming week. The seventh day will be your Sabbath; that is your time to reflect, give thanks, and enjoy your life.

My hope is that the scriptures I have chosen will inspire you to read additional verses that precede and follow the designated verse. This will lead to a desire to pray for insight, wisdom, and courage that will break the strongholds of worry and fear.

After six weeks, a final challenge for your future is offered. Worry and fear in thought and deed are learned and with God's strength can be unlearned. However, learning anything new, particularly when it replaces past habits, takes practice and consistency. Eliminating bad habits is more likely to succeed when you are developing new habits with a new plan, as well as praying for insight, wisdom, and courage to break the strongholds of worry and fear.

This six week devotional will inspire you to pray, encourage you to cast your cares, plan, and take appropriate action while relying on the Lord. Let that still small voice guide your path as you run the race set forth for you by your heavenly Father.

Enjoy the journey with its peaks and valleys, trusting that God loves you. Just as He has brought you through trials in the past, He continues to work on your behalf. Setbacks may occur, but you must believe that they are simply setups for a more fruitful future; a future without limitations. Persist but be patient. You won't regret it.

WEEK ONE, DAY ONE
CAST YOUR CARES AND WORRIES ON GOD!

1 Peter 5:7

Cast all your anxieties on him, because he cares for you.

This verse means that you are not alone in your circumstances. Worrying does not help. Tell yourself to let God help!

It is a known fact that fifty percent of what we worry about never comes to pass. Of the other fifty percent, one third of our worries do not manifest themselves to the degree that we anticipate. We have, in other words, catastrophized about the situation we were facing.

Another third, are not within man's control. They are the "acts of God", so to speak, such as natural disasters. The last third, are within the realm of taking care of ourselves, physically, mentally, and spiritually. Yet even those lifestyle practices are no guarantee that we will experience a long, prosperous life. In other words, worry is futile in terms of having any bearing on our futures. Only God knows the long-range plan, and we can relax if we turn it over to him.

I use self-talk to dismantle my negative, self-defeating thoughts and replace them with hopeful, confident thoughts. Instead of saying, "Here we go again," when it appears that something unexpected is going to interfere with my plan for the day, I say to myself "Maybe God's plan is meant to interrupt mine. Perhaps he wants to replace it with His plan for my day. Or it could be, that He is protecting me from an unknown circumstance that could cause far worse consequences than this simple interference to my day."

Our words are powerful weapons in the battles we face in our everyday lives. You can say them to yourself, speak them out loud, or write them down to be saved for future use. They are reminders that God loves you unconditionally.

1 Peter 5:7

Write this verse in a notebook, on sticky notes, or in the space provided:

_____

_____

Create three simple two- or three-word sentences to use in order to distract your negative, worrisome thoughts. E.g.: Stop It! or God Loves Me!

1. _____

2. _____

3. _____

Begin your gratitude journal or use the space provided to list five specific things that you are grateful for today. E.g.: My lab results came back and they were negative; my sister called to invite me to dinner on Sunday.

1. _____

2. _____

3. _____

4. _____

5. _____

WEEK ONE, DAY TWO
KNOW THAT THE LORD HAS A GOOD PLAN FOR YOU!

Jeremiah 29:11
For I know the plans I have for you, declares the Lord, plans to prosper you and not to harm you, plans to give you hope and a future.

This is my life verse. It always works to recite it when I feel discouraged or am beginning to worry about my future. I realize that worrying has never, in and of itself, changed the outcome of my situation. I never want to forget the times that God walked through the valleys with me and brought me out into a future blessed more abundantly than I could have foreseen or deserved. God is so merciful. His blessings humble me. I pray that my pride will not cause me to try to work things out without His direction. I remind myself that worry is a contradiction of faith.

Keeping a prayer journal is a way to reflect back on how your prayers have been answered, or not…. God hears our requests. His timing is perfect. He may say no to your requests or yes or not yet. Have you ever actually been grateful that a prayer was not answered in the manner that you thought you needed?

Perhaps a relationship would have ended up in a disaster had that prayer been granted. Perhaps you would not have met your soul mate or had the children that you now cherish. Perhaps you realize that you simply were not ready to handle the request you made.

Don't neglect to write in your gratitude journal. Remember to simply write down five specific things that you are grateful for at the end of the day.

With all journals, write down the date and the day of the week. It is likely that you won't stop with just five things. This is especially true when you are thankful for people, your church, your country, and that the Lord saw you through another day. Praise God!

Jeremiah 29:11

Write this verse:

_____

_____

Before you go to bed, recite this verse three times to remind yourself that your worrisome circumstances will pass and the Lord will be with you always.

In your journal, draw a line down the center of the page (or use the table provided below). In the column on the left, list specific needs that you are asking God to meet. Needs are specific things that you require in your life. Wants are things that you would like to have but can be deferred. This should help you differentiate when developing your Needs list. In the column on the right, list prayers that have been met in the past even if the answers were "no" or "not yet".

Needs	Previously Answered Prayers (list dates)

WEEK ONE, DAY THREE
GOD ANSWERS

Psalm 86:7

In the day of my trouble I call upon you, for you answer me.

My friend asked, "What does this verse mean?" I responded, "That you are not alone. Let God help you." It is such a waste of energy to worry or fret about things over which we have no control. And yet I find myself being a "slow learner" regarding this very habit. Behavior is learned and therefore it can be unlearned. I have taught my students that concept and yet I, myself, fall back into that habit.

The triggers that create my tendency to worry are loneliness, tiredness, hunger, and anger. If I can catch myself fretting or trying to fix something when I am in any of those four states of mind, I can prevent futile use of valuable time. Catching yourself is the key! Instead of worrying or thinking negative thoughts, I can do what is in my best interest such as eating something nutritious, getting some much–needed rest, listening to uplifting music, connecting with a loved one, and most importantly, praying. In other words, let God be God.

I find that if I quiet myself and listen, I will receive an answer from the Holy Spirit who is sent to me by God to guide me and protect me 24/7. This turns my exhaustion and/or loneliness into hopefulness and peacefulness. It creates a spiritual hunger within me to grow closer to the Lord. It dissipates my anger because the closer we draw to God, the easier it is to love unconditionally as He does. We can trust that He answers us with provision for our needs.

Psalm 86:7

Write this verse:

_____

_____

With your eyes closed, take a deep breath and blow it out slowly. Take another one, and one more. Quiet yourself and think of ways to gain peace. How will you avoid those triggers that cause you to worry or fret? Open your eyes and list specific steps to use in each of these categories.

Loneliness... I will _____

Tiredness... I will _____

Hunger...   I will _____

Anger...   I will _____

WEEK ONE, DAY FOUR
TRUST IN GOD

Proverbs 3:5-6

Trust in the Lord with all you heart and lean not on your own understanding. In all your ways acknowledge Him, and He will make straight your paths.

I don't know about you, but I tend to be very analytical. I have this need to know and understand everything before I make decisions or take action. When that doesn't happen, I find myself asking "why?" after the fact.

Why did I do or say that? Why didn't I do what that still small voice seemed to be urging me to do? This scripture is posted on my bathroom mirror as a reminder to not only trust the Lord, but to look to him for guidance about even the smallest choices such as how to spend my time or with whom to spend it.

I no longer fret about things over which I have no control. I have stopped being concerned about what other people think of me. Nor do I worry about making mistakes. I have been given the insight to first consult with Jesus, my confidante and my counselor.

Before my feet hit the floor in the morning, I give thanks for this beautiful day, which obviously has nothing to do with the weather since the blinds are still closed—as are my eyes, actually.

I ask to be blessed, provided opportunities to serve Him, and protected from harm or evil. I ask for wisdom and discernment, but I do not expect to understand everything that the Lord leads me to do or warns me not to do. This daily habit definitely takes the worry out of my day.

Make it your habit to give thanks before your feet hit the floor and again at bedtime. It is said that it takes twenty-one days to foster a new habit. Don't keep feeding or fueling the old habits that started your mornings with negative expectations. Trust that habits (thoughts) are learned and can be unlearned. Notice how your attitude has changed midway (21 days) through this six-week journey.

Proverbs 3:5-6

Write this verse:

_____

_____

_____

List 3 concerns that you are turning over to the Lord, and name someone with whom you will share your plan. That person will become your accountability partner for the remaining weeks of this challenge. Select someone with whom you can be totally honest and whom you admire in terms of their attitudes of hopefulness and trust in the Lord.

1. _____

2. _____

3. _____

My accountability partner will be:

_____

Name and Relationship

WEEK ONE, DAY FIVE
THINK ABOUT GOOD THINGS

Philippians 4:8

Whatever is true, whatever is honorable, whatever is just, whatever is pure, whatever is lovely, whatever is commendable, if there is any excellence, if there is anything worthy of praise, think about these things.

People ask me how to use self-talk effectively. I explain that what works for me is to say, "Stop it" out loud and distract myself immediately. Driving the car down dark, lonely, threatening roads used to be where I found my mind wandering. Even on the way to work or on the way home, I worried or doubted the lighted path of my future. In order to distract myself from these negative thoughts, I would turn on a favorite Christian musical CD. If I sang along it was even more helpful. That is probably because I used more than one sensory channel: listening and speaking!

Being human would frequently result in those thoughts creeping back into my mind. This time I would slap my little cheek and say, "Stop it; I mean it." This required more action, which usually included listening to a Joyce Meyer CD and telling God I was giving the "challenge" to him. Notice, I did not say "problem." Psychologists reframe words to represent a more positive, hopeful solution.

I would like to tell you that the challenge has always been met and the habit ended. The truth is that Satan likes to creep back into my life as he does yours. However, I am confident in my skills and most importantly in my Lord. My lifestyle has changed and I find myself traveling from place to place mostly in my golf cart rather than my vehicle.

Being in the golf cart helps me to notice the beauty of God's creations much more easily.

I picture the precious faces of my grandchildren and great grandchildren.

I focus upon the flowers, trees, birds, and other animals.

I recall how the Lord has protected me and my loving husband on our mission trips, through bouts of illness, and even during impending danger.

These thoughts and images provide me with reminders that God will provide. History tells me that he always has, even in my bleakest moments.

Lastly, I have memorized scriptures that specifically speak to my concerns. And I know that I can access many others on my iPhone or in my Bible. I copy them and put sticky notes on my bathroom mirrors and the visors of my vehicle. All of these strategies help me to remember that I don't need to worry about tomorrow and I can find joy this very moment, regardless of my circumstances.

Philippians 4:8

Write this verse:

_____

_____

_____

_____

Think of people who reflect these virtues and pray for them.

WEEK ONE - WEEKEND CHALLENGE

Memorize one of the first five verses of this sixty-day challenge. Re-write it in the space provided as well as on sticky notes or other small pieces of paper. State the name of the verse before and after repeating the verse to yourself. Repeat it to yourself throughout the day.

If you are not accustomed to memorizing scripture, select a short verse. Recite and write! Write how this verse can change your habit of worrying, fretting, dreading, and fearing. Vow to put your plan into action!

_____

_____

_____

Next to the words on the left, or in your journal, write a thought that comes to mind and vow to keep it! Focus on these things this coming week.

TRUE... _____

HONORABLE... _____

JUST... _____

PURE... _____

LOVELY... _____

COMMENDABLE... _____

EXCELLENT... _____

WORTHY OF PRAISE... _____

WEEK TWO, DAY ONE
DO NOT BE ANXIOUS

Luke 12:22-25

And Jesus said to his disciples, Therefore I tell you, do not be anxious about your life, what you will eat, not about your body, what you will put on. For life is more than food, and the body more than clothing. Consider the ravens: they neither sow nor reap, they have neither storehouse nor barn, and yet God feeds them. Of how much more value are you than the birds! And which of you by being anxious can add a single hour to his span of life?

When I read these verses, they serve as a valuable reminder that God provides. He provides for our spiritual and emotional needs, not simply our physical needs. Living amidst all of his natural beauty in Florida, I am able to visually experience the magnificence of his creations. I am hearing impaired so I am particularly grateful for the devices I wear that allow me to hear the sounds of waterfalls, wind chimes, birds chattering, praise music, and most of all the voices of my loved ones and friends.

Being in touch with nature and the still small voice of the Holy Spirit, I have learned to focus on the blessings I do have and not the materialistic items that I lack. I also do not have to ask the Holy Spirit to speak up and face me when he speaks. That's meant to be humorous, but for those of you who are in my position or who live or work with those of us who can't hear easily, you understand the frustration of which I speak.

Life is fragile. By being anxious or worried, I know that I cannot add a "single hour" to my life span. Using the valuable time allotted to me to become more Christ–like is my daily prayer. Taking control over that which is within my control is the only way I can honor Jesus and prepare myself for spending eternity reunited with loved ones and walking with my Lord and Savior.

Luke 12:22-25

Voicing your faith publicly will reinforce your desire to replace worry and fear with trust in God. How many opportunities have you had today to acknowledge your faith to someone?

List the opportunities you had today, whether you actually took the opportunity or not.

_____

_____

_____

When we serve others, in word or deed, it takes our minds off of ourselves. Vow not to overlook opportunities to speak out tomorrow! Our lives are like vapors. We fret over things that will not matter in the future. We put off things that we may regret later. We are simply passing through this world. It is not our final resting place. Don't waste your energy on futile worries.

WEEK TWO, DAY TWO

DEVELOP THE FRUITS OF THE SPIRIT

Galatians 5:22-23

But the fruit of the Spirit is love, joy, peace, patience, kindness, goodness, faithfulness, gentleness, self-control...

Being Christ—like takes the focus off of ourselves. Developing the characteristics of Jesus, known as fruit of the Spirit, will refocus our thoughts on the needs of others. We live in a society with self-absorbed people whose actions are often driven by self-serving motives. People who perhaps do good but for secondary gain. Jesus asks us to develop his characteristics with altruistic hearts. When you put God first and other people second, leaving yourself in third place, your depression and worries will subside.

On our recent mission trip to the Apache Christian boarding school and reservation, I was reminded how quickly and easily children respond to love and return love so unconditionally. If we can learn to love as little children love, and reach out in kindness and gentleness, we can trust and embrace God's love. Seek ways to honor Him by reaching out to those in need. Let's be a beacon of light to those who live in a dark world.

This doesn't mean that your life will be perfect and that you won't face trials and tribulations as the saying goes, but you will feel more energized, and your days will be filled with purpose.

In areas where God has not honored my prayer request, I have learned that those needs have actually changed over time. Now I simply pray that His will be done and know that I can rely upon his promises to protect me.

Galatians 5:22-23

In order to become more Christ–like, circle three of the fruits that you will prioritize tomorrow. State the small steps you vow to take to foster growth in those areas:

Love   **Joy**   **Peace**

Patience   **Kindness**   **Goodness**

Faithfulness   **Gentleness**   **Self-Control**

WEEK TWO, DAY THREE
TRUST GOD TO MEET YOUR NEEDS

PSALM 23

The Lord is my shepherd; I shall not want.
He makes me lie down in green pastures.
He leads me beside the still waters.
He restores my soul.
He leads me in the paths of righteousness
For his name's sake.

Even though I walk through the valley of the shadow of death,
I will fear no evil,
For you are with me;
Your rod and your staff they comfort me.

You prepare a table before me,
In the presence of my enemies;
You anoint my head with oil;
My cup overflows.

Surely goodness and mercy shall follow me
All the days of my life,
And I shall dwell in the house of the Lord forever.

One Sunday many years ago, I was walking through my living room and I caught an interview on Christian television. It was between Dr. Robert Schuller and his daughter who had lost her leg in a motorcycle accident at the age of thirteen. He asked her what sustained her in the darkness, in the dampness, in the ditch that night. She answered that it was the 23rd Psalm. I thought to myself, if it was good enough for that girl, it is good enough for me. I promptly looked it up in my Bible and memorized it.

Later, when needing to feel the closeness of God, I began to visualize each phrase as I spoke it. I remember picturing myself as a young girl with long braids sprawled out on the hill of a green pasture. I could not picture myself as an adult woman for many years thereafter. But always, Jesus was approaching me with a lamb in his arms and another at his feet. He reached down and took my hand to walk beside a babbling brook.

I cannot begin to express how peaceful that felt and how encouraging it was to know that he would be walking beside me throughout my days and protecting me from my enemies.

I must admit that I had difficulty picturing the valley of the shadow of death. But I heard a message from a television evangelist describing that valley as being the threat to the sheep as dusk occurred. I've heard that sheep are dumb and dirty. I, for one, no longer want to be easily lead into dangerous territory where I can fall off the cliff so to speak.

My last thoughts regarding this prayer are that I have named my angels, Goodness and Mercy. And they are with me, I know. I had a lovely, very efficient office manager by the name of Ruth. I can't tell you how often a check would come in the mail just in time to pay a bill that was due immediately. I would say, "Praise the Lord and praise to my angels, Goodness and Mercy." She would ask, "Why do you do that? I billed it!" I would respond that she did not deliver it that day. Don't get me wrong. God's timing is not always our timing. We simply need to do our part and pray about the things over which we have no control.

Speaking this prayer and picturing each phrase is the best remedy for insomnia. I do this each night prior to turning off my light. You cannot repeat it twice without falling asleep or back asleep in the middle of the night. Why do I say repeating it twice? Because being human, you might be inclined to become distracted the first time through. So, begin again and you will find that you can sleep without worrying, whether it is regarding your family's needs or your own; your circumstances or theirs.

Let Go and Let God do His job in them and in you. He is still on the throne. Believe and receive!

Psalm 23

Memorize, memorize, memorize! Visualize, visualize, visualize!

Follow my lead and recite and visualize each phrase of this Psalm. It will ensure peaceful abandonment of your negative thoughts and sleep that you need to restore your energy. If you need to read it, that is fine. But the sooner you memorize it, the sooner you can close your eyes and visualize.

List at least 3 times that God walked with you through a bleak season in your life. Put an asterisk beside it if you felt the presence of the Lord. If you only realized afterward, state how long after that insight occurred

_____

_____

_____

_____

_____

WEEK TWO, DAY FOUR
HAVE FAITH AND WAIT ON THE LORD

Isaiah 40:31

They who wait for the Lord shall renew their strength. They shall mount up with wings "like eagles"; they shall run and not be weary; they shall walk and not faint.

We have been talking about reciting and visualizing the 23rd Psalm and how it provides comfort, courage, and contentment. This verse emphasizes the value of persisting while waiting on the Lord. It suggests resting and a time of renewal.

The Sabbath Principle reminds us to take one day a week, just as God did, to rest and meditate on the good things the Lord has done for us. It is even better to use an hour a day to reinforce those wonders. Your season of life may not allow you an hour to yourself to focus totally upon Jesus. Perhaps you are responsible for small children, someone with a disabling condition, or a busy business. However, you can chat with Him throughout your day. Some people like to use coffee time in the early morning hours to converse with or read about Jesus. Some people say no to lunch with friends in order to "lunch" with the King. Others prefer to close out their day in this manner to prepare for sleep and find hope for tomorrow. Whichever style you embrace, remember to pause and ponder where you are at this moment in time. Even though you aren't where you want to be, perhaps, you can still be grateful that you aren't where you used to be.

Perhaps you have had a horrible childhood, filled with abuse, neglect, abandonment, or other evil. You may be saying, this is all well and good for those of you who can recall all of God's blessings but as for me, I can't recall them. If that is you, do not let your past define your future.

In spite of not having had a loving earthly father or mother, you do in fact have a heavenly father that you can call your hero. He was there with you even when you did not know it. You are his kid and he is waiting for you to run to him. Don't worry. He loves you just as you are. You can "rest" assured of that.

Isaiah 40:31

How can you physically and emotionally (stop worrying!) get more rest in order to do what you can do to become stronger in your faith? Remember that God will do what you can't!

1. _____

2. _____

3. _____

How can you develop patience to wait on God's timing? List a few options that you will try this week. (E.g. Read the Word.)

_____

_____

_____

_____

_____

WEEK TWO, DAY FIVE
MAINTAIN HOPE IN GOD

Hebrews 11:1

Now faith is the assurance of things hoped for, the conviction of things not seen.

Faith is not wishful thinking. It is confidence that God is with you and will see you through whatever lies ahead. With this scripture in mind and its truthfulness in your heart, you can begin to live today knowing there is no reason to worry about tomorrow. Just as you have faith that the sun will rise tomorrow in spite of the darkness that encompasses you in the middle of the night, you can rest assured that God's plan will unfold for you, in His timing.

Timing is often the crux of the challenge. Notice again, I am eliminating the word "problem" from your vocabulary and your mindset. It is human nature to want to have our prayers answered in the manner that we desire at the time that we request them. But our timing is not God's timing and He can see around the corner, so to speak, whereas we often have tunnel vision.

Tunnel vision is having a Plan A without a Plan B. Plan A may be very useful, well formulated, and God–centered, but that doesn't mean that it will come to fruition or at least not now. The question is whether you will allow this setback to stifle your faith, suppress your joy, and make you stumble or whether it will foster your passion, perseverance, and patience.

You can choose to wait on the Lord if you believe your plan is according to God's calling for your life. In that case, it doesn't mean that you don't need to stand still. When God says He is with you as you walk through the threatening times of your life, He isn't saying you should sit there. Moving forward with baby steps may be preparing you for the time that the Lord says "Yes" to your plan.

He may not perceive that you are ready to receive the blessing at this time. Keep gathering knowledge of His word and stepping out in faith. Listen to the still small voice that provides wisdom and discernment as to whether you are actually on the right path. And if your direction is confirmed, challenge yourself to stay the course.

Hebrews 11:1

Write this verse:

_____

_____

_____

Do you struggle with tunnel vision? Do you forge ahead without developing alternate plans as well? Do you neglect to pray for guidance prior to implementing your plan? Is the plan consistent with God's plan for your life?

List two short-term goals (3-6 months). They might be in the areas of faith and fitness. Be sure to pray that the Lord will give you the self-discipline to accomplish them. How will you measure your success? (E.g. Pray as you walk a mile three times a week for 13 weeks; in the second 13 weeks, walk two miles three times a week. Read five psalms and one proverb each day for thirty days. Read the four gospels over the next sixty days to be reminded of Jesus' promises.) These are simply examples of how to develop concrete, measurable goals. I am not saying that Fitness needs to be combined with Faith goals. It is simply offered as an example. Goals could be related specifically to offsetting the habit of worry. Examples have been offered in previous commentaries.

Faith _____

Fitness _____

WEEK TWO - WEEKEND CHALLENGE

Memorize one of the five verses presented this past week. Re-write it in the space provided as well as on sticky notes or other small pieces of paper. State the name of the verse before and after repeating the verse to yourself. Repeat it to yourself throughout the day. If you are not accustomed to memorizing scripture, select a short verse or one that you are familiar with.

My verse of the week:

_____

_____

_____

_____

_____

Looking back at Galatians 5:22-23:

What small steps have you taken so far to foster growth in the three areas that you prioritized?

1. _____

2. _____

3. _____

If you implemented those steps, how has it made you feel?

What do you plan to do next? Underline whatever applies to your thoughts:

Continue to foster growth in those areas.

Add three more fruits to work on in order to become more Christlike.

Both of the above plans.

If you did not implement any steps this week, what goals will you work on in the coming week?

_____

_____

_____

WEEK THREE, DAY ONE
BELIEVE THAT PRAYER MOVES MOUNTAINS

Mark 11:23-24

Truly, I say to you, whoever says to this mountain, be taken up and thrown into the sea, and does not doubt in his heart, but believes that what he says will come to pass, it will be done for him. Therefore, I tell you, whatever you ask in prayer, believe that you have received it, and it will be yours.

Moving a mountain was a metaphor in Jewish literature for doing what was impossible in the natural. But according to the Words spoken by Jesus, those who believe in God can be confident that the impossible can be accomplished.

Believing, however, was not sufficient without requesting what you need from the Lord. Prayer is a powerful tool in overcoming doubt and worry. Worship can take the form of singing praises to God Almighty or listening to Christian music.

It is important to ask with godly motives. Even when we do good things, if the incentive is to receive secondary gain, it is a sin. What secondary gains have you desired in your heart? Recognition? Attention? Financial reward? Respect? Reflect honestly upon these common goals and ask for forgiveness. Realign your requests with a pure heart and you will find answers to long-awaited prayers.

When we trust God to meet all of our needs and ask for those things that would be in accordance with his will for our lives, we can be assured that we are heard, understood, and answered.

Don't give up on healing, physical and emotional, or repairing and restoring relationships. Don't think that because you live from hand to mouth that it always has to be that way. Do believe that God keeps his promises and He promises that you will belong to him forever. With a heavenly father like that, nothing can rob us of our destiny.

Mark 11:23-24

Fill in the blanks:

Truly, I say to you, _____ says to this mountain, be

_____ up and _____ into the sea, and does not _____

in his _____, But _____ that what he says will come to

pass, it will be _____ for him. Therefore, I tell you,

_____ you ask in _____, _____ that you

have _____ it, and it will be _____.

What an encouraging message! We are all special to God. Mark says "whoever" which is a reminder to us to ask for God's favor. Mark says not to "doubt" in your "heart". This means that our knowledge must travel from our heads to our hearts.

Ask yourself if your heart is pure. Do you want that mountain (obstacle) removed in order to gain something that is greedy or selfish in nature?

Write a simple prayer in the space provided. Ask that your prayer be answered so that others will see the glory of the Lord. Most of all, maintain an attitude of gratitude. Better to have some of your request granted than not to pray and have no request to be granted.

_____

_____

_____

WEEK THREE, DAY TWO
ASK AND RECEIVE BLESSINGS

Matthew 7:7-8

Keep on asking and it will be given you; Keep on seeking and you will find; keep on knocking and the door will be opened to you. For everyone who keeps on asking receives; And he who keeps on seeking finds; And to him who keeps on knocking, the door will be opened.

Have you asked for your circumstances to change? Have you worried that if they don't change something terrible will result? Do you simply sit and fret when you think about the future if it is a repeat of the past and the present? Have you given up on praying because to your knowledge, you haven't received an answer?

Why do I say "to your knowledge"? Because, God is working in our lives even when we do not recognize it. He needs us to trust in Him and to do what we can do while he does what we can't do. We need to eliminate the word "try" from our vocabularies. Remember the Nike motto that simply says, "Just do it!"? When you insert the word try in your pledge to face something ahead or do something that is worrisome, it implies that you might fail.

Taking baby steps puts you ahead of where you used to be on the way to going where you want to be. Keep on keeping on. God didn't say to ask once. He said to keep on seeking. Don't give up. Keep God first in your thoughts and through your day.

Keep a running dialogue with him. People used to think that you were delusional if they looked over at you in the driver's seat of your car and saw your lips moving. However, with the hands-free laws in many states, drivers have their phones attached to their dashboards. They are on speakerphone.

You can be on speakerphone with God. He can hear you. Let your lips move and, if you are at a red traffic light, let your arms wave. Listen to that gospel music and praise him without regard of what other motorists think.

Remember that the door that God opens may not be the one you are asking for or expecting. He works in wondrous ways. He may provide you with an opportunity that you could never have prayed for because of its magnitude. He is an awesome God.

Matthew 7:7-8

The key words repeated in these verses are _____ _____.

That is right. Keeping on is required of those who believe in and trust in the Word of the Lord.

Have you doubted that God hears your prayers? You just completed a prayer request. State the purpose it will serve for your prayer to be answered.

Have your prayers not been answered in the past in a way that actually means "not yet"?!

Circle: **Yes** *or* **No**

Have your prayers not been answered in a timely manner?

Circle: **Yes** *or* **No**

Looking back, write down what purpose it may have served God to delay the answers to your prayers:

_____

_____

Have you been glad that in His Wisdom, He responded as He did?

E.g.: God's plan for my future did not line up with what I requested. I have been blessed abundantly!

E.g.: The relationship or career opportunity I was seeking was not according to His will!

WEEK THREE, DAY THREE

DON'T SETTLE

Genesis 11:31-32

And Terah took Abram his son, Lot the son of Haran- his grandson, and Sarai- his daughter-in-law, his son Abram's wife, and they went forth together to go from Ur of the Chaldees into the land of Canaan; but when they came to Haran, they settled there. And Terah lived 205 years; and Terah died in Haran.

Why did I select this passage? To encourage you not to worry about your future but also not to settle for less. Worry is always about the future. It may be your immediate future or far reaching future. But it definitely is about your future. It is a form of anxiety, and the more you learn to focus your thoughts on the present, the less you tend to concern yourself with future events over which you have no control.

That is not to say that you should not plan for the future. We all need goals that are consistent with our perceived needs and our values. But notice that while Terah did not worry about following God's plan for his life and the lives of his family, he settled for less by only going as far as Haran. He set out for Canaan and died at the age of 205 in Haran.

We don't know why he didn't just stop there prior to moving on to Canaan. We don't know anything about his lifestyle? We do know that he settled for less.

I urge you not to settle for less than God's hope for your life. He has given us free-will which means we can chose to hear from him and abide with his desires or we can decide to limit our futures by our human abilities. It is known that teachers who have high expectations for their students tend to obtain better results than teachers who only expect their students to perform average. Expectations for ourselves need to be realistic but perhaps higher than we have reached in the past. If our expectations are too high, we may destine ourselves to fail and view ourselves as failures. On the other hand, if our expectations are too low, we are simply saying that we have poor self-esteem or we are afraid of failure. A failed experience does not make us a failure. Ask any professional athlete.

Lastly, remove the word "can't" from your vocabulary. That word suggests that you have failed before you even begin to meet the challenge ahead. Look back on your life and see if there have been times when you regret settling for less. Pray that the Lord will speak to your heart and instill a renewed trust in his plan for your life. Stoke the fire, the passion, that "will" lead you to enjoy the journey to your God–given destiny.

Genesis 11:31-32

Do you recall taking the easy way out? If yes, how old were you?

Have you settled for less instead of pushing yourself toward your original goal? If so, were you influenced by others or was it a choice you made on your own?

Circle: **Others (Who?)**   **Yourself**   **Why?**

If so, has it been satisfying or do you regret not pushing through the obstacles you perceived to be too great?

If possible, given your current circumstances and resources, describe a plan to continue that original journey with modifications. E.g. You wanted to go into mission work in Zambia but settled for a business or teaching degree that would provide a guaranteed income and support for your family.

I am privileged to be friends with a couple who have dedicated their lives to serving the Africans in Zambia and raised six biological children in the course of their ministry.

Then there is the story of Dr. Paul Osteen who was a surgeon and gave it all up to become a missionary doctor primarily in Zambia. This was put on his heart at the age of twelve when visiting Northern Rhodesia (Zambia) with his father, Pastor John Osteen. He did not foresee that he would be a surgeon but that he would return to help the natives some day.

WEEK THREE, DAY FOUR
LOVE YOUR NEIGHBOR

1 John 4:20

If a man says, I love God, and hates his brother, he is a liar. For he that loves not his brother whom he has seen, How can he love God whom he hath not seen.

Worry is a self-absorbed disorder of the mind. If you are worrying about yourself and your circumstances, you really aren't trusting God and won't notice or attend to loving or serving your neighbor.

Who exactly is your neighbor? According to the story of the Good Samaritan (Luke 10:30-35.), as described by Jesus, your neighbor is any person that crosses your path. Your neighbor may not reside close to you. Your neighbor may personally interrupt your plan for your journey. If you are worrying about yourself, you are likely to be too distracted to notice the need of "your neighbor".

Jesus said that the two greatest commandments (Matthew 22:37-38) are to love the Lord with all your heart, soul, and mind and to love your neighbor as yourself. This sounds very much like the Golden Rule, does it not? Do unto others as you would have them do unto you?

When you love someone, you want to stay connected. In this age of technology, it may not be the sound of their voices that you hear but the sound of their texts! You might follow their lives by viewing videos and pictures on Facebook. Some of their remarks may not be personally directed at you such as Twitter. You have choices to comment back, give them "likes" or respond with symbolic pictures. And don't forget the opportunity exists to have face time with grandchildren to build bonds that bridge the geographical distance between you.

What means do you use to lessen your worrisome thoughts? Do you stay in close proximity to God?

Indirectly, you can journal, or more directly you can pray alone or with others. You can sing his praises. You can fellowship with other Christian brothers and sisters. Lastly, you can position yourself comfortably outdoors and absorb the beauty that God has placed before you.

Make a commitment to get your mind off of yourself and do something unexpected for someone else. Do it for someone who would not expect you to respond to their need. If their need is for comfort, send them a card or take them some soup. If they just need to be heard, listen! You will feel encouraged and blessed from being a provider of God's love.

1 John 4:20

To get your mind off of yourself and focus on the needs of others:

Make a list of who exactly you see as your neighbor? Write their Names (if you know them) and beside each name identify the Relationship. Beside the name state exactly what you can do for this person either anonymously or directly.

E.g. Ashlee Smith- my hairdresser. Tip her 50% and give her crayons for her 6-year-old daughter.

Nationally televised ministry- Send a donation toward the purchase of a water well or another immediate need and pray for the recipients.

Church of your choice- Participate in or support a short–term mission trip. Support may be in the form of prayer, supplies, or financial support toward a person who is going on the team.

WEEK THREE, DAY FIVE
LOVE YOUR ENEMIES

Luke 6:27-31

But I tell you who hear me: Love your enemies, do good to those who hate you, bless those who curse you, pray for those who mistreat you.

Jesus commands us to love everyone and not do things out of spite. Let God be God and do not seek vengeance on your own. When we are mistreated repeatedly, we may develop the condition known as posttraumatic stress disorder (PTSD). We may fear the future based upon previous abuse. We may have a specific person or situation that feeds this disorder or triggers emotional responses. We may resent people who were aware of our abuse and did not intervene in our behalf. Some people may blame God for not getting us out of our circumstance even when we prayed for relief.

Who are our enemies? They aren't always individuals who have directly harmed us or our loved ones. What is true is that direct contact breaks down barriers created by stereotypes.

I am reminded of a recent short–term mission trip to an Eastern European satellite campus of an American Christian college. My husband and I felt led to initiate short-term mission trips for seniors from our church in Florida. Working on behalf of this college, our team of 12 spent 16 days cooking, repairing, cleaning, gardening, hosting student tables, and praying together in the outskirts of Vienna Austria.

Traditionally, there is a campfire on a hill where students strum a guitar and sing hymns in their own languages. We, American, alternate doing the same. The students also provide testimonies of their faith, rejection by family members who won't tolerate religious freedom, their persecution by government or other institutions, and even arrests for gathering together to worship Christ.

At this particular campfire, one of our team members stood up and declared that he was an international pilot who had been a fighter pilot in the United States Air Force. He went on to tell the students that he trained young men to kill Russian soldiers. He added that he wanted to tell us all that he can now say he loves the Russian students. We were speechless and a hush came over that site. Suddenly, a middle–aged Russian student stood up and told the same story indicating he had trained Russian pilots to kill Americans. He turned to our friend and told him that he loves him too.

They embraced. I don't believe in coincidences, do you? In my opinion, that circumstance was orchestrated by God so that we could demonstrate our unconditional love for one another.

If God has not provided you relief from your painful circumstances, be hopeful that he has a good plan for your life whereby your experience will have prepared you for your opportunities.

Luke 6: 27-31

Can you identify a barrier that has been caused by fear?

If so, state what the fear is and in your opinion, how it was developed.

Describe the barrier created by that fear?

Have you removed that barrier? If so, what steps did you take?

If not, what allows you to maintain that fear?

List any beliefs you have changed and indicate whether the original belief was based upon personal experience, the media, or the influence of others.

_____

_____

_____

_____

WEEK THREE - WEEKEND CHALLENGE

Memorize one of the five verses presented this week. Re-write it in the space provided or in your journal. Place it on sticky notes beside the others you have written. Be sure to state the name of the verse before and after repeating the verse to yourself. Meditate and write about why you selected these particular verses.

_____

_____

_____

_____

_____

You are mid-way through this six-week challenge. Ponder about how you have changed your negative thinking. What strategy have you implemented that helps you to modify your thoughts?

Think on this: Hope is expecting good things to happen. Worry is a contradiction to Faith. And Faith is diminished without Hope!

WEEK FOUR, DAY ONE
DO NOT FEAR

Isaiah 41:10

So do not fear, for I am with you; do not be dismayed, for I am your God. I will strengthen you and help you; I will uphold you with my righteous right hand.

Fear is learned and therefore can be unlearned. There have been many studies regarding actions taken or not taken as a result of fearful, sometimes painful, experiences. At times, actions have produced consequences that were out of human control. Once those consequences became anticipated, the fear was exacerbated thus immobilizing the subjects of the studies. Just because a negative or terrifying consequence occurred in the past, doesn't mean that it will still exist in the future. It can, however, result in an irrational fear that has become generalized from just one specific circumstance: An example would be if you generalize that all men/women cannot be trusted simply because your experience has shown that a particular person could not be trusted.

This is not to say that you should not fear, rather that you should face your fear by acting in accordance with your wisdom and faith in the Lord's protection. When we surrender to God's will for our lives, we may fear that He will send us to Africa. Well, guess what? From my experiences in Africa, the natives fear that they could be sent to New York! In other words, fear can be a result of stories we have heard or read when we in fact have had no personal experience to counter those perceptions. Let me add that fear is not a sin.

You may feel called to serve the poor, the needy, or the oppressed, but just can't fathom having the strength, knowledge, or resources to do so. However, God can provide you with exactly what you feel is lacking, once you commit to serving Him by serving others.

I am reminded of my two trips to a farm in Zambia. The missionary family, consisting of Mother Rachel, Father Jim, and two teenage daughters, lived on a 2000-acre farm located beside a narrow river. The farmhouse needed renovation. A village was nestled on the other side of the river and my missionary friends employed the natives to work in the garden. In exchange, they received a wage, fresh vegetables from the garden, clean water from the well, and a weekly Bible study in their language with translators.

Our team had the privilege of teaching vacation Bible school at two locations. One week we taught in a church in town, behind a wall with a gravel courtyard. The next week we taught in a remote village where children carried siblings on their backs while their mothers worked in the fields. I worried that I would not be helpful and that the natives would not trust us. I prayed for guidance and faced my sense of inadequacy. In that village, we provided lunch bags filled with hygiene items to the older girls. Those children by our standards had nothing but in fact they believed they had everything because they felt loved. I might add that they were not deprived of food or shelter. They simply had no stuff, such as toys, that we as Americans value.

Isaiah 41:10

How do you believe your greatest fear was learned? Could it be that your mother held that fear?

Do you face your fear or cower immobilized or run the other way, so to speak?

Complete the following statements:

1. I have faced it by _____.

2. I have overcome it by _____.

3. I have stopped in my tracks, so to speak. I feel _____.

4. I have run the other way and it has _____.

Have you surrendered God's will for your life and if so has that reduced or eliminated your dread or fear?

If not, are you ready to surrender and who are you ready to tell?

WEEK FOUR, DAY TWO

TRUST IN GOD'S POWER

11 Timothy 1:7

For God did not give us a spirit of fear, but of power and of love and of calm and well-balanced mind and discipline and self-control.

This verse speaks for itself. What more is there to say? We are not meant to be timid or cowardly but to be forthright and courageous. When faced with a fearful situation, I usually will ask myself, what is the worst that can happen? Then I consider whether I could survive that outcome. I realize that I might not like it, but I believe that I could survive almost anything that I am called to face: humiliation, failure, loss, regret, or worse.

I believe this because I can reflect back on all the times that God has seen me through the bleakest seasons of my life. Remembering his goodness and mercy bolsters my determination to see the situation through. I think of the times that my mind exaggerated the threat that I allowed myself to believe. I see how with the support of the Holy Spirit, I was able to battle those thoughts and feelings and work toward a positive resolution of my situation.

I also understand that God knows the future while we do not. When my husband passed away quite unexpectedly, I could not foresee that God's plan would bring me a Godly widower with whom to spend the rest of my life. I never doubted, however, that there would be a light at the end of the tunnel. I clung to the 23rd Psalm, persisted with my responsibilities, and waited patiently for the next chapter of my life to unfold.

God brought me through darkness and sorrow to complete the race he has set forth for me. I must say that I experienced guilt in several areas. One is that of survivor guilt. Why was my poor husband's life cut short while mine, at the age of forty-nine, was spared? Why was my life enriched by a new relationship, new extended family, and new church family?

My new widowed husband helped me to deal with that by directing me to Romans 8:28, which says, "all things work together and are for good to and for those who love God and are called according to His design and purpose."

Do not live with guilt without disclosing your thoughts or sins to another Christian brother or sister. If there are sinful thoughts that you are obsessing over, repent by asking God for forgiveness. Rest assured that he will grant you his forgiveness. Guilt can fuel fear and keep you from putting your past behind you and moving ahead each day.

If you have gotten off course and no longer can envision the finish line, trust in your heavenly father. Vow to follow His son and the direction of the Holy Spirit. Whether or not your earthly father offered you love and comfort in times of trial, rest assured that God will never leave you or forsake you.

11 Timothy 1:7

What have you dreaded in the past?

Did the circumstance you dreaded reach the dire outcome you expected?

If not, what did you learn from it?

If so, is there anything you can do to prevent the likelihood of that situation occurring again?

What coping skills have you learned as a result of surviving that experience?

If it is not within your control, what can you do to prepare in the natural and endure or survive?

How would prayer help? Faith?

Believing that God is and will always be with you!

Do you have a calm and well-balanced mind?

What would you advise yourself and other to do to obtain it?

Are you self-disciplined?   *How do you work at it?*

WEEK FOUR, DAY THREE
TRUST IN GOD'S PROTECTION

Psalm 27:1

The Lord is my Light and my Salvation;
Whom shall I fear or dread?
The Lord is the Refuge and Stronghold of my life;
Of whom shall I be afraid?

Sometimes when we dread something, we fail to prepare to the best of our ability.

Whether it is an unpleasant or painful medical procedure, or a personal or legal proceeding, dread is just one step beneath fear. Do you have the habit of dreading things that are scheduled in the future? When did you first begin this behavior and under what circumstance? How did it turn out?

I used to dread mammograms, dental work, testifying as an expert witness in a Court of law. I dreaded two–day road trips, completing graduate school written exams, and verbal confrontations of any kind. The more I prepared for these circumstances, the more successes I experienced. I found myself thinking, "Cast your cares and let go so God can be God."

You might ask how can you prepare for mammograms, dental work, or even surgeries?

I have found that if I remove myself mentally, I can tolerate these procedures more comfortably. There are two imageries that work for me. If I am undergoing anything medical, I visualize the phrases of the 23rd Psalm and view myself beside still waters with my friend, Jesus. If I simply must focus somewhere outside of myself for a few seconds or moments, I imagine myself walking on a beach with a lighthouse as my focal point. I tap into as many of my senses as I can, such as what I can see, hear, smell, or feel. I usually see dolphin in groups of three and shrimp boats in the far distance. I hear the surf and the birds at play. I feel the sand beneath my toes and the water against my ankles. I smell the freshness of the air.

The story of the virgins waiting for their bridegroom is a great example of the importance of being prepared. Half of them saved enough extra oil for their lamps in the event he arrived in the darkness of night. The other half failed to do so and wanted to borrow oil from the virgins who had prepared. Don't wait until the last minute and risk consequences that can be avoided. Stay in the Word. Listen to the Holy Spirit for wisdom and discernment, and trust that God is beside you always. He will light your path as you take baby steps and face the future with boldness.

Psalm 27:2

The lighthouse is a reminder that the Lord is my light!

What symbol is your reminder?

What natural setting reminds you of the Lord's blessings and offers you peace?

What prayer or Bible verse provides you comfort?

WEEK FOUR, DAY FOUR
BE STRONG AND COURAGEOUS

Joshua 1:9

Have I not commanded you? Be strong, vigorous, and very courageous. Be not afraid, neither be dismayed, for the Lord your God is with you wherever you go.

The word dismayed is translated in Webster's dictionary as discouraged. It is easy to be discouraged after suffering a setback, unexpected perhaps. Setbacks are often obstacles that are thrown in our paths when we are moving forward toward a goal. The more often we have been faced with setbacks, the less likely we are to keep going.

Victory may be just around the corner yet we will not get there if we retreat to where we began. Changing a habit like smoking, drug use, alcohol abuse, or overeating can involve a series of failed attempts. We need to accept responsibility for those attempts and not blame others or our circumstances. But it is known that the more times you fail means the closer you are to the time that you will succeed.

Ask anyone who has relapsed in those areas and you will hear stories of how they overcame those failures and what they do to maintain success once it is achieved. First and foremost, is the use of prayer and allowing God's power to thrust you toward eliminating that negative, self-defeating habit? Secondly, they have sought support from others who have modeled their ways of winning the battle as well as those who are facing the same challenge, perhaps at different points of their journeys.

Pray, journal, and show gratitude for tiny breakthroughs each and every day. Use positive self-talk that pats you on the back and this will lessen your tendency to be dismayed or give up. Rely on a prayer partner with whom you can be open and authentic.

There is a song whose lyrics ring in my ears at times of weariness and discouragement. The words say to let the weak say I am strong and let the poor say I am rich because of all the Lord has done for me. And lastly, to give thanks. Be strong in faith and you will ultimately soar.

Believe that you are richly blessed, and you will prevail against all obstacles. Give thanks that you are not where you were yesterday or an hour ago, for that matter.

Joshua 1:9

God did not give us a timid spirit! Think back at what you feared as a child under the age of ten. What was the outcome?

Did the outcome matter in the long run?

What did you fear when you were a teenager?

What was the outcome?

Did the outcome matter?

Did you retain that fear in adulthood?

Even if the worst came to pass, it is not an excuse not to face your giants again. You now have experience and skills that you did not possess as a child.

WEEK FOUR, DAY FIVE

FAITH BRINGS PEACE

Mark 4:39-40

*He woke up and rebuked the wind and said to the sea,
"Peace! Be still!"*

Then the wind ceased, and there was a dead calm.

*He said to them, "Why are you afraid?
Have you still no faith?"*

This is a familiar story found in the Gospel of Mark. Jesus had instructed the disciples to leave the crowd behind and take a boat to the other side. A great windstorm arose and the waves beat into the boat. Jesus was asleep in the stern and they woke him up. They asked him if he didn't care if they perished.

Can you relate to this story? Have you followed what you believed to be God's will or the direction of the Holy Spirit only to have faced what you perceived as insurmountable obstacles? Did you pray fervently and receive the equivalent of a small miracle? Did you repeat that process and doubt that God could intervene when, in fact, he has done so in the past? The disciples were right there beside him when he performed miracle upon miracle. Yet they doubted that he would rescue them in this frightening time of need.

How many times do we have to receive blessings before we learn to believe in the promises of God? He promises to never leave us or forsake us. Do we even recognize the blessings or do we take credit for accomplishing difficult plans on our own merit?

Perhaps God allowed you to flounder in order to prepare you for his good plans for your future. Perhaps you weren't mature enough in your faith or knowledgeable enough to reach your goals. Now may be the time that God says Yes to your prayers to accomplish something great in your life. Now is the time to stop doubting God and stop fearing failure.

Do you think your cup is not just half empty but totally void? See that cup as half full and not half empty. Fill your heart with gladness and let him walk with you and guide you to your destiny. Don't keep making the same mistakes that leave you weary and helpless.

Don't let it take 40 years in the wilderness to complete an eleven-day journey to the Promised Land. Be obedient, faithful, and hopeful that God's yes means yes-now.

Mark 4:39-40

Where can you go to meditate and listen to the Holy Spirit?

Jesus has provided us this still small voice to deepen our faith. Don't neglect to take the time to hear the message of the Lord.

Jesus can calm the storms in life if we keep our trust in Him. Have you prayed fervently and received the equivalent of a small miracle? A great miracle?

Describe them:

_____

_____

_____

_____

WEEK FOUR - WEEKEND CHALLENGE

Memorize one of the five verses presented this week. Re-write it in the space provided or in your journal. Place it on sticky notes and review the first three weekend verses.

_____

_____

_____

_____

When you read the four verses that you selected, do you gain any insight into steps you can take to replace worrisome thoughts?

Fearful thoughts?

Plan to step out and take a small step in faith this week. For example, that conversation that you have been putting off keeps going round and round in your head. Don't worry about the approval of others; simply say what it is that the Lord has put on your heart to be said. The obsessive thinking will disappear and you will no longer having those thoughts and feelings hanging over your head, so to speak.

If you need to face a frightening situation that would not necessarily be frightening to others such as flying or testifying in Court or performing in a musical: pray, plan, and do it!

WEEK FIVE, DAY ONE

RECEIVE REST

Matthew 11:28

*Come to me, all you who labor and are heavy-laden and
overburdened,
And I will cause you to rest.
I will ease and relieve and refresh your souls. (AMP)*

Are you most fearful when you are most exhausted? Jesus reminds us to take time to focus upon him rather than racking our brains on how to face the battles alone. What is true is that God won't do for you what you can do for yourself. Therefore, it is imperative that you pray for guidance from the Holy Spirit in your quest to know whether you are doing all that you in the natural, physically, can do.

We are told that in spite of being followers of Christ, we will face trials and tribulations in this life. The question is whether, because you believe in God's promises, you will prevail with hope in your heart. This requires us to stop, rest, and listen in the midst of lengthy days and dark nights. We must stop the negative thoughts that create doubts in those valleys. We must see these trials as useful as we run our race or at least maintain the belief that we will experience insight on the other side of the mountain.

How can trials be seen as useful and how can we be content as we go through or anticipate them? We need to recall the times that God allowed Jesus and his followers to face persecution, disloyalty, and isolation. When they prevailed, they experienced a deepened faith and trust in the mercy, love, and loyalty of God. Recall times when Jesus' friends experienced disappointment in him yet soon came to see that his actions were purposeful and in their best interest.

The story of raising Lazarus from the dead (John 11:1-44) is a prime example of how God will allow us to suffer with a greater goal in mind. By raising Lazarus after he had been dead for four days, it left no doubt in the minds of the people who were present, that Jesus performed this miracle. Therefore, their faith was strengthened or restored. It didn't mean that Jesus felt no compassion for the suffering Mary and Martha as they witnessed the death of their brother. God is with us through our suffering. He is with us at all times. Mary and Martha never doubted Jesus' ability to keep their brother from dying. They simply could not understand until afterwards why he chose not to come right away. Understanding his ways is not a requirement, faith is!

God tests our loyalty and favors us when we step out in faith. This requires us to pray first, take action, even baby steps, prior to receiving His blessings. The Holy Spirit will lead us to do what is right and convict us when we act according to our own will. We simply need to take time to quiet our minds and rest in the assurance of God's presence in our lives.

Matthew 11:28

Come to me, all you who _____ and are _____ _____ and

_____ _____, And I will cause you to _____.

I will _____ and _____ and _____ your souls.

Do you recall a time when pure exhaustion played upon your fearful thoughts?

Explain: _____

Did you wake up with a renewed sense of courage?

Did you place your hope in Jesus?

If so, did you find peace?

How?

Have you lacked understanding when faced with an unpleasant circumstance that God did not rescue you from or intervene quickly?

Have you gained insight later?

What were those circumstances?

Describe: e.g., Jesus didn't come to heal Lazarus. Instead, he raised him from the dead. This was purposeful on His part but misunderstood by Martha and Mary.

_____

_____

_____

WEEK FIVE, DAY TWO
BELIEVE AND RECEIVE

John 6:35

Jesus said to them, "I am the bread of life; Whoever comes to me shall not hunger, And whoever believes in me shall never thirst.

What is it that we really fear? Is it hunger? Have you ever actually felt your stomach rumble or ache from lack of food? Have your lips been parched from lack of clean water? I personally have never experienced such lack. However, I have personally seen the result of it in children and women of Africa. I have viewed it on Christian television programs. It touches our hearts and should put our fears in perspective.

Do we want to be penniless and homeless? Of course not. Is it a true threat that needs to be addressed or is it a futile thought when our finances don't seem to stretch this week?

Can we be content with less than what our flesh desires? Or are we consumed with envy toward those with more material blessings?

Don't get me wrong; there is a season for everything. Some people are able to participate in both of these alternatives. Some people support missions and still enjoy leisurely trips and perhaps beautiful homes. Being affluent, financially, is not a sin. Money and material possessions that take precedent over a close relationship with God is deemed sinful. You cannot serve two or more gods. Only the one God can diminish your fears and bring you the spiritual nourishment that you crave. After all, if God is with us, whom shall we fear?

Make a list of needs and a list of wants. Separate your needs list into those needs you require in a relationship and those needs that you value in life. Separate your wants lists in the same manner. Wants are defined as those things that you can defer. Do you need material things or has respect, affection and intimacy with God topped your "needs" list? Has God taken the highest priority? Have you ever even thought about your personal relationship with God when you count your blessings?

In terms of wants, I would love to go to Hawaii or take a river cruise down the Danube with my husband for our twentieth anniversary. But when weighing the importance of these choices, I find that I would prefer to put my limited resources into another short-term mission trip. At the very least, by prayer and/or financial contributions, I can support those who are willing and able to go. In my own small way, I am helping them to spread God's love to those who are in need. This lets our light shine so they will know about the God that we represent.

John 6:35

Refer back to your needs list from Week One. In your journal or in the space provided, you may desire to modify your list to reflect your personal and spiritual growth in the past four weeks. Remember that needs are those things that you believe are necessary to your well-being. If you recognize God as the center of your life, your time and resources should reflect that principle. E.g. to put daily time with God ahead of other plans for the day.

Complete the same task for your wants list. Remember that wants are those things that you realize can be deferred.

What wants can be deferred in order to honor God? e.g., Instead of spending money on a movie and dinner with friends, donate new toys to an organization that provides toys for needy children.

Needs	Wants

How do you believe you might be blessed if your needs and wants are in line with God's divine plan for your life?

WEEK FIVE, DAY THREE
RISK ALL FOR WHAT IS RIGHT

Esther 4:14

For if you keep silent at this time, relief and deliverance will rise for
the Jews from another place,
But you and your father's house will perish.

And who knows whether you have not come to the kingdom for such
a time as this?

Esther, the Queen of Persia, was a beautiful and courageous heroine. She risked her life to save a Jewish nation from destruction. Her cousin, Mordecai, had raised her and warned her not to let the King know that she was of Jewish heritage. She then became the queen on her own merit. Mordecai informed her of a plot to destroy the Jewish people. She devised a plan to approach King Ahasuerus and request a favor of him. She knew that this was very dangerous and he could order that she be put to death. She was able to provide the King with information of a traitor in his palace. He, in turn, fulfilled her request to revoke an order to have the Jews obliterated.

The book of Esther only contains ten chapters. It is a powerful love story that encompasses Esther's courageous, faithful love of her people and her God. Faith coupled with loyalty, to her cousin and her country, motivated her to face her fear and think not of what her personal fate might be. She planned carefully and believed that God would empower her to make a quite outrageous request of the King.

Is your personality style that of being proactive or reactive? A proactive approach to pending doom is to act as Esther acted. She was not impulsive and did not give in to worrying about "what if". What if the King refused to believe her when she told him there was an evil man in his palace regime? What if he thought she was the terrible one who had deceived him by not telling him that she was Jewish? He could have her put to death or exile. What if he thought that her request was inappropriate given her position?

A reactive approach to solving a dilemma such as Esther faced, is to take a "wait and see" attitude. Do you tend to react once a situation has arisen rather than taking measures that might have avoided the outcome from occurring at all?

If you have usually viewed the future as gloom and doom but found that what you feared has not actually been a threat, then perhaps a wait and see style is the best approach. Has your judgment in the past been clouded or valid? Did you successfully weigh the threat and not minimize it or exaggerate it? If so, then praying, listening, and taking action may be what you are called to do and why you are where you are at such a time as this.

Don't let this divine purpose in your life pass you by. You may be the instrument for the salvation of your children, grandchildren, or other loved ones. Face the fear and know that you are not alone. God is always with you and doesn't expect you to face anything that you are not equipped to complete.

Esther 4:14

You are encouraged to read the entire book of Esther.

If you have answered the questions in my daily commentaries, you should begin to recognize the style you have adopted for dealing with stressful or fearful situations. You may recognize the need to modify your approach to fulfill your God-given destiny.

Esther's plan involved several strategic steps. She didn't impulsively rush into the King and state her demand. Putting your plan on paper implies that it is a goal not a dream. Sharing your plan with a trusted person increases the likelihood of achieving it.

Do you have a sense that this is the time appointed for you to risk stepping out for a cause you believe in? If so, develop a plan and a time line required to accomplish your goal and list the steps here:

Plan: (E.g. Put resources into participating in a mission trip.)

Timeline: (E.g. Next twelve months.)

Steps: (E.g. Contact individuals who develop mission trips.)

Goals Accomplished: (E.g. Completed mission trip.)

WEEK FIVE, DAY FOUR
RELY ON GOD

Psalm 91:2

*I will say of the Lord, He is my Refuge and my Fortress, my God;
on Him I lean and rely and in Him I trust.*

Notice that this verse does not say that you think of the Lord as your refuge and your fortress. It says, "I will say of the Lord...." This means that we should tell others that we believe that God is our safety net, our protector, and our strength. Are you too timid because you fear that you will be ridiculed, criticized, or even rejected?

If we expect God to protect us against our enemies and to provide us with a safe place in which to rest, then shame has no place in our lives when it comes to proclaiming his love.

He hears our prayers and he knows our doubts. If Jesus knocked on the front door, would you be embarrassed to introduce him to your family or guests? Probably not. This is not any different than letting them all know who sustains you in your troubling times and whom you love the most.

If you lean on and rely on Him, isn't it fair to share where your strength comes from with your friends? When you say it, it will actually reinforce your beliefs and lift your burdens. Aren't relationships supposed to be "two-way streets"? If the only time God hears from you is when you need something from Him and need it urgently, it does not qualify as a mutually respectful relationship. You would become weary if you were treated like that by those who you care about. Those friendships generally go by the wayside. They may have been useful at a different stage of your life but they no longer serve any purpose. Even if they were there for you in a crisis, don't forget that you and your friends weren't in that foxhole alone.

Don't look back and beat yourself up for the times that you see that you were unfaithful to God or neglectful of your relationship. God gives us the grace, which is forgiveness and power, to move forward. You can lean on Him and trust that he will never leave you or forsake you. Make amends to the God who loves you unconditionally and let the world know that you have not and can not make it on your own.

Remember and shout out your blessings. Be thankful that you do not live in a nation where you would be persecuted for declaring your faith in God, Jesus, and the Holy Spirit. Do not take your freedom and free will for granted. You may just be the light that reflects God's glory to a needy world.

Psalm 91:2

Rewrite this Psalm in your journal, on a sticky note, or in the space provided:

_____

_____

_____

Underline two words that most describe what the Lord has provided to you.

Circle two other words that impact you the most and describe how these words can enable you to dismiss your fears.

_____

_____

_____

_____

WEEK FIVE, DAY FIVE
STAY COMMITED

Ruth 1:16

*And Ruth said, Urge me not to leave you or to turn back from
following you;
For where you go I will go, and where you lodge I will lodge.
Your people shall be my people, and your God my God.*

Naomi and her husband and two sons left Jerusalem and settled in
Moab where their sons married Moabite women. Naomi's husband died
followed by both of her sons. Her daughter-in-law, Ruth, insisted on
accompanying Naomi back to Jerusalem to build a new life. Naomi had
kinsmen there and Ruth became employed in the fields. As the story
unfolds, Boaz, the owner of the fields and kinsman of Naomi, took
notice of Ruth. She went from gleaning in the fields to owning the fields!

Not only that, but Ruth and Boaz' son, Obed, later begat Jesse, who
begat King David. The moral of the story is that when you act in
kindness, such as Ruth did by not abandoning Naomi, God will notice.
And out of your losses and poverty will come new beginnings, peace,
and prosperity. That is not to say that you will become the great
grandparent of a king but that you will receive more blessings than you
could have asked for or expected.

Naomi obviously had earned the admiration of her daughter-in-law. She
was viewed as a faithful servant of the Lord. However, after all the
tragedy had struck her, Naomi became bitter, helpless, and doubtful of
her destiny. Ruth had no reason to think that by going with Naomi that
she would truly benefit in any way. She could have returned to her
family as suggested strongly by Naomi. She may have feared how she
would be received by Jews who hated the heathen Moabites. Yet she
did this with pure motives to care for this older woman. She did this
without expecting anything in return.

I gave a Women's Devotional Bible to a dear friend, twenty-two years
ago. She was simply facing the normal trials and tribulations associated
with raising children and maintaining her marriage. She read it from
cover to cover. To this day, she calls me Naomi and I call her Ruth. A

couple of decades later, she was faced with the pending loss of her beloved husband, and she not only relied upon the Word of God to sustain her in that darkness, but she also lead her husband to the Lord When he passed away, she had no doubt as to where he would spend eternity. Without her faith, she will say that she could not have survived those last few months as she watched him dwindle away.

This book of the Old Testament may restore your hope and renew your energy to face the future without worry or fear. Ruth and Naomi could not foresee a hopeful future but Naomi's faith never wavered. She encouraged Ruth to keep doing what was right in spite feeling despair Joyce Meyer would be the first to advocate trust in God and doing good or what is right. Don't give into your feelings.

Does this mean that we may not live on earth to see the rewards o future generations? Rewards precipitated by decisions and actions that we take or elect not to take? Perhaps. After all, Ruth never met her great grandson, David. On the other hand, we may give birth to a new life in Christ that blesses us and those we love on this side of heaven.

Ruth 1:16

You are encouraged to read the entire Book of Ruth.

Have you doubted that God was there with you during a particularly trying period of your life?

Has your faith been restored?

If so, how?

Has there been a significant Christian in your life that lead you to or back to the Lord?

Who and how?

Be sure to show gratitude and pray for that person.

WEEK FIVE - WEEKEND CHALLENGE

Circle whom you most identify with:

Esther   **Ruth**   **Naomi**

What is it about that person's life that touches your heart and encourages you?

What is it about their choices that remind you of your own? Good, bad, active, passive, courageous?

What is it about their faith that will provide you courage to plan your future?

WEEK SIX, DAY ONE
BELIEVE EVEN IN HARD TIMES

Habakkah 3:17-18

Though the fig tree should not blossom, nor fruit be on the vines, the produce of the olive fails and the fields yield no food, the flock be cut off from the fold and there be no herd in the stalls, yet I will rejoice in the Lord; I will take joy in the God of my salvation! (ESV)

There have been times, have there not, when anything that can go wrong seems to have gone wrong? There is an old wives' tale that suggests that bad things happen in threes. Have you found yourself literally counting after two such things have happened? Have you told people that you are waiting for that third disastrous thing to occur? I know that I have and so has my husband. At this time of our lives, the negative happenings seem to be related to household matters. The water heater went out at the same time as the garage door opener. The third item was the refrigerator that wouldn't cool. These are minor inconveniences but somewhat costly on a retirement budget. I might add that we didn't sit around simply waiting for these things to occur. Yet we were not particularly surprised, given the age of the appliances.

When more serious things transpire unrelated to material possessions, our worry, fret, and fear genes do tend to kick in. For example, when we receive that dreaded phone call in the middle of the night, about someone near and dear to us, regarding an accident or medical emergency, we never seem to be prepared.

When such experiences have happened more than once, the mere sound of the phone ringing can create anxiety. Being exposed to a disastrous outcome may produce a more serious condition known as posttraumatic stress disorder.

My husband has faced medical emergencies unrelated to cancer, of which he is a twenty-one-year survivor. These emergencies have occurred when I was temporarily unavailable, like not watching him play senior softball in the Florida heat! That translates into dehydration and an ambulance ride to the hospital. He holds the record for 911 calls from the softball diamonds. He also suffered a stroke, with no residual damage, and a heart attack while I was out of state conducting professional business. One remedy for not worrying is to modify your lifestyle to lessen the likelihood of being far away from your elderly relatives. That translates into my sitting through most softball games, only traveling with my husband in tow, and taking care of myself so that I have the stamina to be his caretaker when needed.

The prophet Habakkah reminds us not to give up during times of famine. In Zambia, there are two seasons. One season is very hot with drought. I witnessed that firsthand when I was there on a farm and there had been no rain in five months. The other season produces rainy monsoons. I also witnessed that season. The natives love umbrellas. They use umbrellas in both seasons. They find them to be very functional. During the hot drought, umbrellas protect them from the sun and during the rainy seasons, obviously they protect them from the rain.

Seeds will not produce a harvest if planted near to the expected drought. Likewise, seeds sown too near the rainy season will be washed away. The Africans who work in the fields or own the fields have learned how to farm successfully from experience. They recognize that it really isn't within their human control.

A wise person looks up toward the Lord instead of down toward the circumstances. Looking up means to pray for your harvest, sow the seeds in a timely manner, and patiently wait on the Lord. Take cover to protect yourself and know that God will do what you cannot do. Lean on the Lord and praise Him for who he is, not what he can do for us. Remember to be joyful in the midst of your circumstances and rest assured that God will be there to lead us through whatever we may face.

Habakkah 3:17-18

Have you experienced mild, moderate, or severe post-traumatic stress disorder (PTSD)? If so, identify the cause? (Or write it in your journal).

_____

_____

_____

Have you completely overcome it? If so, what worked for you?

Prayer?   Bible reading?

Christian friends and others?   How?

Family support?   How?

Therapy?   In-patient?   Medication?

Out-patient?   How Long?   Individual?   Group?

If you relapsed, identify the triggers such as smells, sounds, places, people, etc.

What is your relapse plan for the future?

If you still suffer from this disorder, don't give up! Look up toward the Lord!

LEAN ON HIM!

WEEK SIX, DAY TWO
RENEW YOUR MIND

Romans 12:2

*Do not be conformed to this world, but be transformed by the
renewal of your mind,
that by testing you may discern what is the will of God,
what is good and acceptable, and perfect.*

Do you worry because of pressure that is applied to you by your
employer, spouse, family, and friends? Are you afraid of disappointing
them or not meeting their expectations?

Remember, that as a Christian we are in this world but we are not of this
world. We are set aside by God to be bold and step out for Him. This
requires us to discern how we should serve others and still serve God.
God desires that we serve others as his son, Jesus, came to serve us.
Jesus stated that when we serve the least of these, we are serving him;
the least of these being the orphans, the homeless, the widows, the
poor, and the unsaved.

This verse confirms that as normal human beings, with faults and flaws,
we need to be energized to do what is right by renewing our minds. This
means that we need to be reminded by reading the Word of God that
the Lord is the lamp to our feet and the light to our paths. Your load will
seem lightened and your heart will be filled with joy when you keep
your eyes on Jesus. You will not burn out before you finish the race set
forth for you.

Let me caution you not to do too much for those who always appear to
be in need. If there are things they could do for themselves, then you
may be thwarting their growth when you intervene and enabling them
to continue as they always have. At the very least, you are not trusting
God to be God. Your words of encouragement are always appropriate,
but only God can do the work in their minds and hearts.

Romans 12:22

How have you served the least of these?

Did you realize that in so doing, you have served the Lord?

Do you continue to do so?   If not, why not?

Given your change of circumstances, physical or financial, have you revised your method of service? How might that be? E.g. Instead of short-term mission trips to a third–world country, I can serve in Europe, stateside, or through financial support.

Are you or have you been co-dependent? That is, does your joy or happiness depend upon the happiness of someone else, such as your adult child or spouse?

If so, give their needs to the Lord and stop trying to fix them.

Write a prayer and stop doing God's work. Let God be God in their lives!

WEEK SIX, DAY THREE

ASK FOR OPPORTUNITIES

I Chronicles 4:10

Jabez cried to the God of Israel, saying, Oh, that You would bless me and enlarge my border, and that Your hand might be with me, and You would keep me from evil so it might not hurt me! And God granted his request. (AMP)

he name Jabez means pain. Can you imagine a mother naming her son abez? She came up with the name because she bore him in pain. Do ou suppose that other children bullied him so that he would live up to is name? There were two books written based upon this simple verse ı the Old Testament. The first was a devotional written by Bruce Vilkinson, and the second was written by his wife, Darlene Wilkinson, pecifically for women.

efore I share the meaning of this prayer and its application for your fe, I must share the Wilkinsons' story. Bruce and his wife were ttempting to retire to California. However, their plans were thwarted Ime after time. He and his son went on a short-term mission trip to outh Africa to help the natives plant gardens. The Lord spoke to him nd he believed with all of his heart that he and his wife were meant to ve in South Africa. He called her one night and she said, "Please don't ell me that we are moving to South Africa." Basically, he said "Yup." He ame home to Atlanta and through his church was able to generate nancial support and manpower who were willing to go teach the South .fricans how to plant gardens. It is said that you can give a man a fish or a meal or you can teach him to fish for a lifetime of meals.

Iany of us feel as though it is selfish to ask for blessings for ourselves. et if we are not strengthened, what good are we to others? Jabez sked God to bless him by enlarging his territory. For Jabez the prayer /as probably literal. He most likely used the land for his livelihood. For s, it may pertain to opportunities. If we have a servant's heart, then we nay want to expand our opportunities by opening doors to accomplish ur goals. This may require that we gain new knowledge or acquire financial resources or receive support in the form of partnering with people.

It is important that while we are waiting for God to answer our prayers we do the best we can with what we've got. This is known as blooming where we are planted, right?

Be careful not to bargain with God. That is, do not say that if God grant you your prayer, then you will do good things to advance His kingdom on earth.

Pray that he will protect you from evil or those who would want to prevent you from succeeding. I was supposed to teach a workshop on raising awareness of human sex trafficking but the Life Long Learning College for Seniors closed down the month prior to my course. I have stated that Satan did that to limit the knowledge of this evil practice.

Christine Caine and others will not allow their voices to be silenced. God protects us.

This prayer also acknowledges normal human frailties by asking that the Lord keep us from causing harm to anyone else. This is not always a sin of commission but can be a sin of omission. That is, it can either be something that we say or do that is not beneficial to others or something that we fail to do when we know it is right. We pray that our motives remain pure and that we do not get distracted from our mission. With more territory, so to speak, we risk suffering burn out and not having the energy to set realistic goals and not be deterred from reaching them.

Meditate on what you believe that God is asking you to do with the days he has provided to you. Write down your purposes and processes. Then simply set out, if you have not already done so, and begin doing it. The smallest step will be recognized by God even though others may not notice. What you do in private demonstrates to God that you have a heart to serve others without secondary gain. Ask Him to expand your borders. Trust that when He thinks the time is right because your maturity is sufficient to complete the journey, He will answer you.

1 Chronicles 4:10

What requests would you like to make to the Lord, but have not done so? Beside the request, or in your journal, identify what has prevented you and then list your prayer requests? E.g. Feelings of unworthiness.

Name them and claim them, so to speak.

Request: _____

Prevention: _____

Ask yourself what purpose will these answered prayers serve?

How would you describe what good you are now doing for others in the name of Christ?

What you could do when your prayers are answered?

Obey God's commandments, keep on doing good, and wait to receive his blessings.

WEEK SIX, DAY FOUR

SPEND TIME WITH JESUS

Luke 10:38-42

As Jesus and his disciples were on their way, he came to a village where a woman named Martha opened her home to him. She had a sister called Mary, who sat at the Lord's feet listening to what he said. She came to him and asked, "Lord, don't you care that my sister has left me to do the work by myself? Tell her to help me!"

"Martha, Martha," the Lord answered. "You are worried and upset about many things, but only one thing is needed. Mary has chosen what is better, and it will not be taken away from her."

Have you ever felt as if others are taking advantage of you because they are not pitching in and doing their part of the work? Have you ever considered that simply because you see the work as having to be done immediately, it is you who is taking advantage of them by insisting that they use their time to do your bidding?

This story of Martha and Mary demonstrates how one sister tends to fret and is concerned about how others see her while the other sister values the presence of Jesus in spite of what others may think. It was not common for women to engage in a setting of all men let alone to sit at the Lord's feet amongst them. Mary valued the relationship and words of Jesus more than impressing him with the offering of good food and drink. She understood that Jesus loves us unconditionally while Martha expected recognition for the work she was doing for him. Martha invited him into her home without permission of her sister. Yet she imposed her will upon her sister to help her serve him the way she chose to serve him.

Don't get me wrong. Those who labor for the Lord are to be commended. Some of us are Marthas and serve the Lord and those who he loves. However, we must remember that works without faith are useless. And faith is demonstrated by valuing our time with Jesus by reading The Word and quieting ourselves to experience his presence in our daily lives.

Luke 10:38-42

Are you guilty of imposing your will or judging someone else because you believe that what you are doing is more important than what they are doing? Or, that your time is more important to you than their time is to them?

Who might that be? E.g. colleagues at work, family members, church committee members...

_____

Explain the circumstances that lead you to have this belief?

If you are a Martha, has that service mentality interfered with spending quality time with the Lord? If so, how can you adjust your lifestyle or daily routine to develop more time for intimacy with Jesus?

If you are a Mary, do you neglect to take care of the practical everyday responsibilities because they seem to serve little purpose?

Remember that God has you planted where you are and that completing mundane tasks for the love of the Lord is the purpose that you are meant to serve.

List three thoughts in your journal or in the space provided that will assist you in maintaining balance in your routine.

_____

_____

_____

_____

_____

WEEK SIX, DAY FIVE
PRAY AND RECEIVE PEACE

Philippians 4:6-7

Do not be anxious about anything, but in everything by prayer and petition with thanksgiving let your requests be known to God.

And the peace of God, which surpasses all understanding, will guard your hearts and your minds in Jesus Christ.

These two verses should be posted everywhere in your home. Post it on your bathroom mirror, your bedroom mirror, your refrigerator door and on your laptop. Don't forget the visor of your vehicle! If we want to experience peace in spite of our circumstances, then we need to include God in all of our circumstances. He cares about our minor concerns as well as our greater struggles.

Our prayers can simply be dialogue with Jesus and they do not need to be grandiose or repetitive. Giving thanks for the smallest gifts will be noticed by God. That might mean a special phone call from an old friend, unexpected financial reward, or good news about your medical concerns.

Vow to do what you can do first, such as tithing any first fruits received in the form of that first paycheck or monetary gifts. If you are expecting some expense to cost more than it actually does, give that savings to the Lord. We recently had a new water heater installed with no money down and no service charge. It will simply cost ten dollars a month more on our gas bill. The Lord will receive what we estimated that we would be charged by the fruits we will sow for the benefit of others.

We knew this was a God wink. A God wink is when you believe that something good has happened unrelated to luck or chance!

When your mind focuses on what you have rather than what you lack, that sense of gratitude will bring you the patience you need to wait on the Lord's response to your needs.

Be sure to write in a gratitude journal every night. Include the date, da of the week, and of course, the year. Write down five things that yo were specifically grateful for that day. Needless to say, one of the fiv items might be that you are grateful that you got through whatever th day required of you and it is over!

Starting at the end of the journal, turn the journal upside down, the give thanks for the blessings you have received along with new praye requests. Again, date everything so that you can look back and reca your joys, hardships, and needs having been met by our loving, mercifu God. You will have peace in trusting Him.

Philippians 4:6-7

Do you really trust God or is that just lip service? Do you pray about everything and praise Him for what He has provided? (Noted in gratitude journal!)

Have you experienced an unforeseen blessing recently? A God wink!

Did you receive an unexpected financial windfall, a communication from a long, lost friend, or some other unsolicited blessing? Large or Small. Describe it!

How did you respond to that circumstance?

What feelings did it invoke?

What action will it prompt you to take in the near future?

WEEK SIX – FINAL CHALLENGE
KEEP YOUR EYES ON JESUS

Matthew 14:27-31

But immediately Jesus spoke to them, saying "Take heart, it is I. Do not be afraid."

And Peter answered him, "Lord, if it is you, command me to come to you on the water."

He said, "Come." So Peter got out of the boat and walked on the water and came to Jesus.

But when he saw the wind, he was afraid, and beginning to sink he cried out, "Lord, save me."

Jesus immediately reached out his hand and took hold of him, saying to him, "O you of little faith, why did you doubt?"

The disciples were battling a ferocious storm in the darkness of the night. They spied Jesus walking on the sea. They feared him thinking that they were seeing a ghost. Notice that immediately Jesus calmed them down by confirming it was he. Peter wanted proof and requested that he be commanded to get out of the boat and walk to Jesus. Jesus honored his request. As long as Peter kept his eyes on Jesus, he was able to walk to him. When he allowed his thoughts to focus upon the utter impossibility of what he was doing, he began to sink. It is said once again that Jesus "immediately" reached out his hand and saved him. Jesus did not offer sympathy to the terrified Peter. Instead, he chastised him for doubting the supernatural power of the God of the universe. They returned to the boat and the disciples did indeed acknowledge him as the Son of God.

This message is meant to remind us that first of all, we have to get out of the boat in order to demonstrate our faith and trust in Jesus. Secondly, to not lose focus and retreat out of fear. We must not allow our fear to stifle our footsteps. We must not look back or be diverted from the sidelines. The course set out for us requires us to keep our eyes on what lies ahead.

This does not mean that we should set unrealistic goals that may not be in line with what God's plan might be for our lives. But nothing ventured, nothing gained. Sitting in the boat or on the fence, so to speak, will not change our circumstances.

We should take moderate risks that are not immoral or illegal. Moderate risk takers are said to have the highest self-esteem and the greatest self-control. Low risk takers are afraid of failure and will put up with the status quo. High risk takers are usually impulsive with no clear vision of what steps they need to take. They may have dreams without measurable goals. Baby steps are not in the vocabulary of a high risk taker.

Moderate risk takers, on the other hand, understand that they may face some setbacks but they should not view themselves as failures. Failed experiences teach us to modify goals and builds resilience and patience.

The principles presented to you during this six week walk are intended to bolster your self-confidence, change your negative thinking patterns and encourage you to get out of the boat. Face the future with renewed faith and hope in God's promises.

Pray for direction and listen to the response of the Holy Spirit. Answers may not be audible but will present themselves through resources such as other people, thoughts, dreams, and most importantly The Word. Lastly, develop discernment and insight.

FINAL CHALLENGE

How can you keep your eyes focused on what lies ahead?

At times of insecurity, anxiety, or fear, what has helped you?

How do you classify yourself? Circle one of the following:

low risk taker   **moderate risk taker**   **high risk taker**

Has that worked for you?

What goals have you met with that style of approaching life's challenges?

Do you need to modify your practice of risk taking? Why?

Restate your existing goals, and set new goals based on the insight that you have obtained over the past six weeks. Remember to keep your eyes on Jesus.

In your journal, monitor your progress on a weekly, monthly, quarterly, and annual basis.

Remember: Be grateful that although you may not be where you want to be, you are blessed to not be where you have been!

Worry, Fret, and Fear... No More! Enjoy the journey.

INDEX BY BIBLE VERSE AND TOPIC

27545403R00076

Made in the USA
Columbia, SC
25 September 2018